Ways into Technology

Making with Paper

Written by Claire Llewellyn

W
FRANKLIN WATTS
LONDON•SYDNEY

First published in 2008 by Franklin Watts
338 Euston Road
London NW1 3BH

Franklin Watts Australia
Level 17/207 Kent Street
Sydney NSW 2000

Copyright © Franklin Watts 2008

Editor: Julia Bird
Design: Shobha Mucha
Photography: Paul Bricknell (unless
otherwise credited)
Consultant: Pam Bolton, design and technology adviser

A CIP catalogue record for this book
is available from the British Library

ISBN 978 0 7496 8085 5

Dewey Classification 745.54

Printed in China

Picture credits:
p.7: (clockwise from left) istockphoto © Joe Potato;
Shutterstock © Diana Rich; Shutterstock © Arunas Gabalis;
© Shutterstock © objectsforall; istockphoto © blaneyphoto;
p.8: (top) Shutterstock © Andrei Nekrassov; (bottom)
Shutterstock © Kmitu; p.9: (top) Shutterstock © Kmitu.

Every attempt has been made to clear copyright. Should
there be any inadvertent omission please apply to the
publisher for rectification.

Thanks to our models: Tilly Lumsden, Amrit Paul, Phoebe
Price, Jordan Robinson and Mimi Ward

Franklin Watts is a division of Hachette Children's Books,
an Hachette Livre UK company.
www.hachettelivre.co.uk

Contents

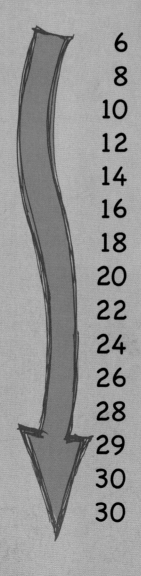

Paper products

Paper is a very useful material. We can use it to make many things.

Tilly's card is made of paper.

Phoebe is playing with a paper party blower.

Have a look around you. Lots of things we use are made of paper.

Can you think of any other things that are made of paper?

Which **paper?**

There are many different sorts of paper. They are all good for making things.

These boxes are wrapped in shiny paper.

Cardboard is a type of paper. It is used to make boxes and packets.

Wallpaper is thick. It is used to decorate walls. It can have patterns or pictures on it.

Amrit wants to make a Christmas card for his friend. It is important that he chooses the right kind of paper.

Which do you think he will use?
Turn the page to find out.

Making a card

Amrit chooses coloured card because it is bright and stands up by itself.

He folds it in half to make a hinge. Now the card can open and close.

Hinge

Amrit cuts out three circles of white paper to make a snowman. He glues them on to the card.

Toolbox
- Card • Paper • Scissors • Glue
- Pipe cleaners • Cotton wool

Amrit sticks on pipe cleaners for the snowman's arms.

He makes eyes, a nose, a hat and some buttons with pieces of coloured paper.

Amrit finishes the card off by adding balls of cotton wool for snow.

Safety note:
Take care with scissors. They are very sharp.

Shaping paper

Paper is easy to shape.
When you fold, roll or twist a sheet
of paper, you change its shape.

Phoebe made this snake by
shaping a piece of paper.

Why not try
making a snake of your own?

Take a piece of paper
and start rolling it
from one of its
corners into a tube.
You will need to roll
it quite tightly.

When you have rolled all the paper into a tube, stick down the end with a piece of tape.

Toolbox
- Paper • Tape
- Coloured pens

Holding the tube at both ends, twist it gently. This will make it into a more interesting shape.

Now use your imagination to decorate your snake with coloured pens.

Making a door

Tilly has made a house out of a cardboard box.

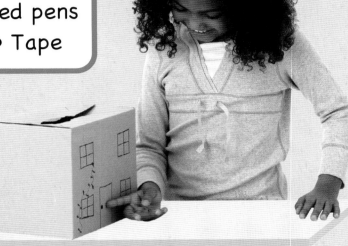

Cardboard is a good material to build with because it is strong.

Tilly has drawn a door on her house.

She cuts out the door to make a hole.

Next, she cuts a piece of card to cover the hole. She sticks it to the house with masking tape.

The tape works like a hinge. Now the door can open and close.

Tilly makes a back door for the house. How has she made this door?

A paper pattern

Mimi is making a coat for her doll. She finds a pattern for a coat on the internet and prints it out on some paper.

Toolbox
- Scissors
- Pins
- Fabric
- Glue

Next, Mimi cuts the pattern out.

Safety note:
Take care with scissors. They are very sharp.

Mimi pins the pattern to two pieces of felt. She cuts around it carefully. Now she has two coat shapes.

She cuts one of the pieces in half so the front of the coat will open.

Mimi sews the coat together, then puts it on her doll.

A paper pattern can be used again and again. What kind of coat could you make with Mimi's pattern?

A game of **skittles**

Jordan is making a game of skittles. He is going to roll marbles down a ramp to knock the skittles over.

Toolbox
- Scissors • Glue
- Cardboard box • Card
- Marbles • Tape

Jordan makes the ramp. First, he cuts off the two narrow sides of a cereal box.

Safety note:
Take care with scissors. They are very sharp.

Jordan sticks the two sides together, one on top of the other. This makes the ramp stronger.

Now Jordan makes the skittles.
He copies a skittle shape on to a piece of card. Then he cuts it out.

How do you think he could make the skittle stand up?
Turn the page to find out.

Knock them down!

Jordan cuts a tab out of card. He tapes it to the skittle shape.

Now the skittle will stand up.

Jordan rolls a marble down the ramp. The marble hits the skittle but doesn't knock it over. What can Jordan do?

Jordan makes a new skittle which is narrower than the first skittle. He adds a tab.

The second skittle stands up but it is not as strong.

Jordan rolls a marble down the ramp. The skittle falls over!

Moving pictures

Books and cards are made of paper.
Sometimes they have moving pictures.

When you open this Christmas card,
a picture pops up.

This book has a tab. If you pull it, the picture moves.

What do you think the crocodile will do if you pull the tab?

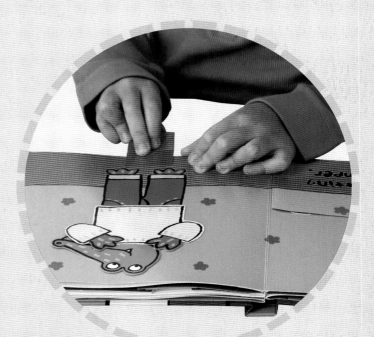

Mimi has designed a moving picture. She has sketched a picture of a cat and a dog.

Which bit of this picture could Mimi make into a moving part? Turn the page to find out.

The **jumping** dog

Mimi is going to make the dog jump up at the cat.

She draws the cat in the tree again on a piece of card. She draws the dog on a separate piece and cuts it out.

Next, Mimi makes a lever. This is the part of the picture that will move. She lays the lever on the picture to check that it is the right size.

Mimi makes holes in the lever and the card. She joins them together with a paper fastener.

Then she glues the dog to the end of the lever. Now the dog jumps up and down!

Safety note: Take care with scissors. They are very sharp.

Try making a moving picture. What would move in your picture?

What do you  know?

Look at the pictures on this page.

Can you describe the paper that has been used to make each object?

Can you think of a reason why each type of paper was used?

Can you match the words in the orange boxes with their description?

Tab

B. A bar that you push or pull to make something else move.

Lever

A. The place where a door or card swings open and shut.

Hinge

C. A strip of paper or material that is attached to something else.

Useful words

cardboard – thick, strong card that is made of paper.

design – to plan and draw something and decide what materials should be used to make it.

fabric – cloth.

felt – a kind of cloth.

hinge – the place where a door or window swings open or shut.

hole punch – a tool for punching holes into paper and other materials.

lever – a bar that you push or pull to make something else move.

marble – a small ball made of glass.

masking tape – strong, sticky tape.

material – something like paper, wood and cloth which can be used to make things.

packet – a small cardboard box designed to hold food and other things.

paper fastener – a pin with a stem that is split into two parts.

pattern – a design that you copy to make something, for example a dress.

ramp – a slope.

scissors – a tool with two cutting blades that is used for cutting things.

size – how big or small something is.

sketch – to draw something quickly.

tab – a strip of paper or material that is attached to something else.

wallpaper – thick paper that we stick onto the walls of a house to decorate it.

Some answers

Here are some answers to the questions we have asked in this book. Don't worry if you had some different answers to ours; you may be right, too. Talk through your answers with other people and see if you can explain why they are right.

Page 7 Cups and plates, tablecloths and napkins, lampshades, books and magazines, bags, games and babies' nappies are all made of paper.

Page 15 Tilly has made the second door by cutting the door out along three sides and folding the fourth side back to make a hinge.

Page 17 You could use the pattern to make any garment that has the shape of a coat – for example, a dressing-gown or a raincoat.

Page 23 The crocodile will pull off his jumper when the tab is pulled.

Page 26 The wrapping paper is shiny. It is used to cover the boxes because it looks nice. The cardboard is strong and thick. It is used because it protects the eggs. The wallpaper is thick and striped. It is used to cover and decorate the walls. The cup is made of strong, waterproof paper. It is used because it can hold drinks without leaking.

Page 27 A = Hinge
B = Lever
C = Tab

Index

About this book

Ways into Technology is designed to encourage children to begin to think about how things are designed and made in the world around us. Here are some pointers to gain maximum use from **Making with Paper**. Working through this book will introduce the basic concepts about paper and how it can be used to design and make things, and also some of the vocabulary associated with it (for example, design, decorate, materials, pattern). This will prepare the child for more formal work in Design and Technology later in the school curriculum.

As you read through the book with children, ask their opinion of each of the products. Would they like to make any of them? If so, would they make it in exactly the same way or can they think of different ways of doing it? Do they make things with paper at home? What kinds of things have they made?

On pages 7, 9, 15, 17, 19, 20, 23 and 25, readers are invited to answer a question or suggest an alternative way of doing something. Ensure that you discuss any answer they give in some depth before turning over the page. Perhaps you could set up other scenarios for the children to predict and discuss possible outcomes. For example, on page 9 you could find a selection of possible papers – tissue, card, kitchen roll, wallpaper – to make a party hat. Which materials would work the best? On page 11, you could try making a card for a different occasion. What kind of design and materials would be best to use?

Pages 26–27 are an opportunity to revisit material in the book. Make sure that children are familiar with the names for all the different kinds of paper, tools, materials and actions used in the book.